CHILDREN AND WAR

Robin Cross

CHILDREN AND WAR

Other titles:

Aftermath of War
Cities at War
Propaganda
Technology of War
Victims of War
Women and War
World Leaders

Cover illustration: A propaganda poster shows a small baby under threat. All sides in the war claimed to be trying to build a better future for their children.
Contents page: A forlorn-looking German boy at the end of the war, dressed in clothes made for a man.

First published in 1994 by
Wayland (Publishers) Ltd
61 Western Rd, Hove
East Sussex BN3 1JD, England

Series editor: Paul Mason
Designer: Mark Whitchurch

British Library Cataloguing in Publication Data
    Cross, Robin
    Cities at War-(Era of the Second World
    War Series)
    I.Title II.Series
    940.54

ISBN 0-7502-1223-3

Typeset in the UK by Mark Whitchurch
Printed and bound in Italy by
Rotolito Lombarda S.p.A.

Picture acknowledgements
Grateful thanks to John Yates for providing all the artwork. Thanks also to the following for giving permission to use their photos in this book: Archiv fur Kunst und Geschichte, Berlin/Image Select cover, contents, 5, 32, 33; Camera Press 6, 10, 23, 29, 38, 42 top; Image Select 18; Imperial War Museum 11; Peter Newark's Pictures 25, 43, 44; Popperfoto 7, 13, 40, 42 bottom; Tass 15; Topham 8, 9, 12, 14, 17, 20, 22, 27, 28, 30, 31, 35, 36 both, 37, 39; Wayland Picure Library 4, 26.

Contents

Introduction

Hinaus mit allen Störenfrieden!

Einheit der Jugend in der **Hitlerjugend!**

An advert for the Hitler Youth. The organization's military image is dramatically conveyed in this propaganda poster.

On 8 May 1945 children in Britain celebrated the end of the war in Europe with street parties and bonfires on which they burned models of the German leader Adolf Hitler. In Germany there was little for young people to celebrate. The country lay in ruins. Hunger stalked the land. Shame and defeat stood outside every door.

For countless children in Europe and the Far East the winds of war blew away the familiar landmarks of family, friends and school. Fathers went off to fight and mothers went into war factories. In Britain, Germany and Japan millions of children were evacuated from the cities to the countryside to escape enemy bombing. By the time the bombs began to fall, many of them had gone back home. They experienced the mixture of terror and excitement that accompanied heavy air raids. In Germany during the last two years of the war thousands of children were actively involved in civil defence against air raids. As a result they saw and experienced many terrible things.

In Britain wartime rationing meant that children from poorer families had a *better* diet than before the war. In Europe however, as the war dragged on, most children were permanently hungry. In Greece, where the Germans stole the food supply, they starved. So too did children in Poland.

The Germans also forced Polish children as young as 12 years old to work up to 16 hours a day in war factories. When the people of Warsaw, the capital of Poland, rose up against the Germans in September 1944, children were involved in fighting. They served as messengers, running through the city's sewers to avoid the bullets of German snipers. In other European countries teenagers played their part in the underground resistance to the German occupiers. Here, we tell the story of one very courageous Belgian girl, Hortense Daman, who not only fought in the resistance but also endured the horrors of Ravensbruck concentration camp.

As the war drew to a close it was the turn of German children to bear arms. Young boys rode off on bicycles to fight Soviet tanks, carrying their rations in school satchels. Many of them were killed. Others were captured by Soviet soldiers.

The most tragic victims of all were the 1.5 million Jewish children murdered by the Nazis. This was perhaps the greatest crime of the war, but the victorious Allies also had the blood of children on their hands: the tens of thousands of German children killed in the firestorms caused by the air raids on Hamburg, Dresden and Darmstadt; and the thousands of Japanese children who were killed by atomic bombs at Hiroshima and Nagasaki or who died of radiation sickness in following years.

Even in the middle of death and despair, in the grimmest circumstances, children found time to play. But often their games reflected the conflict that was ending the security in which they had lived before the war began.

Hunger in Warsaw

In wartime Warsaw Polish children lived on the edge of starvation. One of them was Jaroslaw Ciechanowicz: 'Not far from our house was a hospital, where we used to go and collect potato peelings which we ground afterwards and baked on the stove, and that was our usual meal. We went around hungry, looking for all kinds of impossible and possible things to eat. The easiest to find was vegetation. Once in the hospital we managed to get hold of mouldy bread, which had already been eaten by mice, but it tasted very good.'

An orphaned German boy at the end of the war makes a sad figure in his outsize coat and shoes.

Evacuation

Evacuees wait to board a train at Liverpool Street railway station. Their labels show that they were heading for Lowestoft, a fishing port in East Anglia.

Britain declared war on Germany on 3 September 1939, but the British had experienced their first big upheaval of the Second World War two days before. On 1 September, the day Germany invaded Poland, Operation Pied Piper went into action – the evacuation of women and children from cities threatened by German bombers, particularly London, Liverpool, Glasgow and Sheffield.

The plans had been ready for some time. In the Munich crisis of 1938, when war looked likely, there had been a small-scale evacuation from Britain's cities. Now it was the real thing.

It was a huge operation which had different effects across Britain. There was no large-scale evacuation from some cities – Bristol, Plymouth and Swansea, for example – which were to be heavily bombed in the winter of 1940. Nor did all those who qualified join the evacuation scheme. In London fewer than half of the city's schoolchildren were evacuated in September 1939. In the northern city of Sheffield the figure was only 15 per cent. The British government had planned to move about 3.5 million people to the safety of reception areas in the countryside. In the end only about 1.5 million responded to the official scheme, although many thousands chose to evacuate themselves under their own steam.

Nevertheless, Minister of Health Walter Elliott described the first wave of evacuation as *'an exodus bigger than that of Moses'*. On the move were 827,000 schoolchildren and 524,000 children under school age accompanied by their mothers. There were also 12,000 pregnant mothers and 103,000 teachers and helpers.

The first phase of the evacuation was accomplished by train. The eventual destination of children in London depended on which of the main railway stations was nearest to their homes. If it was Paddington, for example, you were evacuated westward by the Great Western Railway.

Newspaper photographs of the time paint a calm and orderly picture of evacuation. But it was really a frightening experience for many children. Inevitably there was some muddle and confusion. Some children were put on the wrong train. As the children arrived in the reception areas they were scooped up by buses and ferried to different destinations. Because the bus drivers were under orders to move off as soon as the buses were filled, school parties were broken up as the children were driven to different villages. Some never got back together again.

Two little girls arrive at their school ready for evacuation on 3 September 1939. They both carry gas masks in boxes slung over their shoulders.

Some reception areas were swamped with evacuees while others received only a handful. Children often arrived dirty, hungry and homesick to discover that the families with whom they were to stay would take only those who looked neat and tidy. There are some heartbreaking stories. Jean Talbot was an orphan in a children's home in Leeds when war broke out. She and her sisters were evacuated to Greenboro. They walked the streets with the billeting officer, who was responsible for finding them a home, but no one would take them in. Finally they found a woman who was willing to take all the little girls except Jean and her sister Agnes: *'I was eventually taken by a woman who decided that one night was enough and it was back to the billeting officer, and I went where my sisters were. Then I was moved again and my sister Agnes and I were separated. I never saw her again.'*

A sentimental view of an evacuee setting off to a reception area in the countryside. He has labels showing his school, home address and destination, as well as bags of possessions.

Evacuation highlighted the enormous gulf between the social classes in Britain. Most of the evacuees were children from poor areas. Few of them were as well-clothed as Derek Lambert. Their parents had no money to buy suitable clothes for a long stay in the country. Many of the children were taken in by prosperous middle-class families who were shocked by the evacuees and the mothers who accompanied them. Head lice, bedwetting, swearing and smoking were sometimes held up as proof of the low morals of the working class. Jewish and Catholic children were often the victims of ethnic and religious prejudice. In some areas it was even suggested that the evacuees should be separated from the rest of the population in special camps. Many poorer people who took in evacuees accused richer people with bigger houses of avoiding their responsibility to help.

Evacuation was a complicated business which produced homesickness for many children and anguish for their hosts. In contrast others found themselves transported into a world of unimaginable luxury. Thirteen-year-old Bernard Kops and his sister, who came from Stepney, a poor part of London's East End, were amazed at their new home in Buckinghamshire: *'Everything was so clean in our room. We were even given flannels and toothbrushes. We'd never cleaned our teeth until then. And hot water came from the tap. And there was a lavatory upstairs. And carpets…This was all very odd and rather scaring.'* (From Bernard Kops' book *The World is a Wedding*.)

An evacuee is delivered to her new home by a billeting officer. Not all evacuees were lucky enough to be placed in such pleasant surroundings, and some were not greeted with much warmth when they arrived.

In spite of unfamiliar surroundings and separation from their parents, many children adapted happily to life in the country. However, by the early summer of 1940 thousands of them had been taken home. No bombs had fallen on Britain's cities. Many children were homesick, and the government was now asking parents to make a contribution to the children's upkeep in the country. By April 1940 half of the evacuees from London had returned to the capital, where they found many of their schools shut. The education of many children was disrupted during the war years. The schools were reopened, but many suffered bomb damage, or were destroyed, when the Germans began bombing Britain's cities in the autumn of 1940. This led to a new wave of evacuation from the worst-hit areas. A final phase of evacuation began much later in the war, in June 1944, when the Germans began their V-weapon campaign against Britain.

Damage caused in North London by German flying bombs in 1944. Four years after the first great upheaval of evacuation, a new wave was caused by the V-1s and V-2s.

The experience of evacuation had important social consequences. It brought directly home to those involved the class differences that existed in England and the full extent of poverty in the nation's big cities. The eyes of the middle class were opened when they took in evacuees. In contrast working-class evacuees sometimes encountered for the first time the spiteful prejudices of richer people. Evacuation underlined the poverty of the many and the privileges of the few.

Evacuation played a part in shaping the public desire for the creation of a fairer society when the war was over. It not only struck a chord with the public but also had a direct effect on the policy of the wartime coalition government. Even before it had become clear that the war was won, the government had embarked on a programme of social reforms.

The 'Seavacuees'

After France fell in June 1940 Britain was threatened with a German invasion. Offers to take in British children poured in from British Dominions like Canada and also from the United States. The British government introduced a scheme to send children overseas. To avoid complaints that only the children of the rich were able to go abroad to safety, a quota was imposed - three-quarters of the children had to come from publicly-funded schools. By July 1940 over 200,000 applications had been received, prompting the new British Prime Minister, Winston Churchill, to refer to a 'stampede from this country.' The scheme came to an abrupt end when the liner City of Benares was torpedoed by a German submarine. Seventy-three 'seavacuees' died. In all only about 2,700 children were evacuated abroad by the official scheme.

Above: Goodbye Britain. Children and their mothers are evacuated to South Africa, where they should be safe from German bombs, at the beginning of the war.

A boy in the Gulag

A Polish poster urges 'To The Front'. The Poles were defeated within six weeks.

On 1 September 1939 Germany invaded Poland. The Polish armed forces were rapidly overwhelmed. On 27 September the Germans captured Warsaw, Poland's capital. Ten days earlier, on 17 September, Soviet troops had invaded Poland from the east. When the fighting in Poland ended, on 5 October, Germany and the USSR divided Poland between them.

At the time of the German invasion Jerzy Kmiecik was a 16-year-old schoolboy, the son of a schoolteacher in the province of Cracow in southern Poland. Jerzy and his brother Adam decided to leave home and make their way to France. The boys avoided capture by the Germans, but were not so lucky when they found themselves in the Soviet-occupied zone.

Only 300 metres short of the border with Hungary, the boys were taken prisoner by a patrol and handed over to the NKVD, the Soviet secret police. The two brothers were eventually separated and Jerzy began a long journey which was to take him to Soviet Central Asia and, after many adventures, to Britain.

In January 1940 Jerzy boarded a packed prison train bound for the USSR. Each time the train stopped Jerzy watched bodies being carried out and laid in the snow beside the track: *'By the time the journey ended, I must have seen about 50 such bodies and concluded that the death rate on the train must have been about ten per cent. It wasn't until 17 January 1940 that for the first time in 12 days I breathed the air of the outside world.'*[1]

This was the last of the outside world Jerzy saw for a long time. In the USSR he was accused of being a 'capitalist spy'. In the grim prison at Chernigov he was beaten, threatened with execution and subjected to several kinds of torture as his captors attempted to wring a confession out of him.

Jerzy's jailers told him that 'prison is the best university.' He quickly developed a keen instinct for survival in the brutal conditions of the Soviet prison system.

On 28 August 1940 Jerzy was told that he had been sentenced to seven years imprisonment in a labour camp. Because of his youth, the sentence had been reduced to three years. Until his 18th birthday his sentence would be served in a Children's Working Colony.

At the outbreak of war, young girls help to dig air raid trenches in Warsaw, the Polish capital. With so many young men away in the Polish Army, much of this work was done by members of Poland's national youth organizations.

On 6 September 1940, almost exactly a year since he had left home in Poland, Jerzy arrived at the Children's Working Colony near Kiev in the Ukraine. Conditions here were better, but hunger was never far away. (One winter's day Jerzy killed a crow and boiled it up in a tin can for dinner. He did not repeat the experiment.)

As soon as he was 18 Jerzy was on the move again. After a five-week train journey he found himself in the Karaganda Basin in Soviet Central Asia. Here there was a network of labour camps run by the NKVD, part of a vast system of camps set up in remote areas of the USSR during the 1930s by the Soviet leader, Josef Stalin. They housed millions of people, from ordinary criminals to political offenders.

In the Karaganda Basin, Jerzy worked in quarries and on building sites under a blazing sun for up to 16 hours a day. For many prisoners this cruel place was the end of the line. If a man's daily output fell below the required level, his food ration was cut. He was still expected to do the same amount of work on the reduced rations. When he failed, the rations were cut again. Death from malnutrition and exhaustion inevitably followed.

Nikita Krushchev photographed at the front line in 1943. Ten years later he became the First Secretary of the Soviet Communist Party and the most powerful man in the Soviet Union.

Krushchev's bed

The colony where Jerzy worked until he was eighteen produced furniture in its workshops, and one of Jerzy's tasks was to help in the construction of an enormous bed for the First Secretary of the Ukrainian Communist Party, Nikita Khrushchev. In 1953 Krushchev became the leader of the Soviet Union. Jerzy recalled that *'Khrushchev's bed was enormous. The standard beds that we were making for ordinary mortals contained three rows of nine springs. This bed had seven rows of eleven springs. It was big enough for me to lie across it... We all tried the bed for comfort and it was nice.'*[1]

Jerzy's spirit was not crushed by these experiences. He was planning to escape from the labour camp when news of his release arrived. After the German invasion of the USSR in June 1941 an agreement was reached between Britain and the Soviet Union for the release of all Polish political prisoners in the Soviet Union. They were to form a Polish Army to fight Hitler. Shortly after leaving the labour camp, Jerzy saw a long column of prisoners escorted by Red Army soldiers and dogs. All of them were heavily bandaged, some with missing limbs, hobbling as best they could. *'When they came close enough, I realized that they were German prisoners of war. It was not a pretty sight. Quite a number of them, their heads so heavily bandaged that they could not see, were marching with their hands on the shoulders of the men in front.'*[1]

Joining the Polish Army was not as simple as it sounded. Jerzy had no clear idea where it was being formed. Nor did he have the proper documents to travel freely around the Soviet Union.

German prisoners of war are paraded through Moscow, the capital of the Soviet Union, in the summer of 1944. Few of these men ever saw Germany again. After the Battle of Stalingrad, early in 1943, 110,000 German soldiers were taken prisoner. Conditions in prisoner-of-war camps and labour camps were so bad that less than 5,000 of them survived until the end of the war.

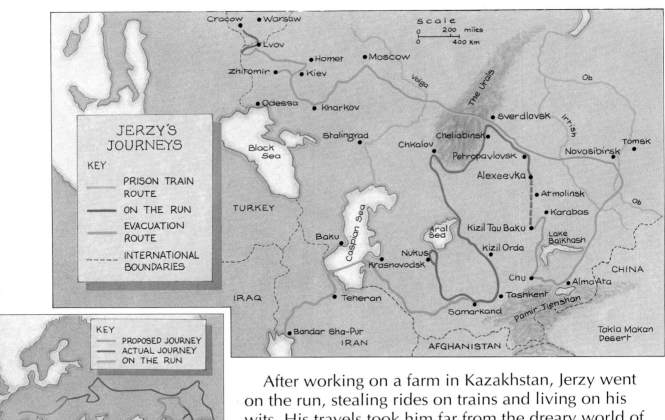

JERZY'S JOURNEYS

KEY

— PRISON TRAIN ROUTE

— ON THE RUN

— EVACUATION ROUTE

---- INTERNATIONAL BOUNDARIES

KEY

— PROPOSED JOURNEY
— ACTUAL JOURNEY
— ON THE RUN

After working on a farm in Kazakhstan, Jerzy went on the run, stealing rides on trains and living on his wits. His travels took him far from the dreary world of wartime Russia to the ancient cities of Tashkent and Samarkand in Soviet Central Asia, where there was life and colour, and hostility to communism.

Travelling without an internal passport, and in constant danger of rearrest and return to the labour camps, Jerzy travelled for five months before chancing on the Polish Army's recruiting centre at Gizhduran. During that time he had covered 8,000 kilometres.

On 16 February 1942 Jerzy Kmiecik became a member of No.5 Squadron, Polish Air Force. On 24 March he left Soviet soil on board a ship which crossed the Caspian Sea to the Persian port of Pahlevi. It was not until August 1942 that Jerzy reached Britain. He became an RAF pilot, flying Spitfires. It had taken him three years and 56,000 kilometres to win his freedom.

Jerzy's brother Adam survived imprisonment in a Soviet labour camp in Siberia and also joined the Polish Army. He fought in North Africa and Italy, and was reunited with his brother in 1946.

A child in the Resistance

On 10 May 1940 Germany invaded Holland, France and Belgium. On the same day Fort Ebn Emael, the linchpin of the Belgian defences, was captured by German paratroops. On 28 May the Belgian Army surrendered. Belgians were to endure a German military occupation until their country was liberated by the Allies in September 1944.

In Belgium there was no shortage of people willing to work with their German conquerors. Thousands of Belgians joined the SS, the main instrument of Nazi terror, and the two police bodies it controlled: the Gestapo (*Geheime Staatspolizei* or Secret State Police), and the SD (*Sicherheitsdienst*, or Security Service). It was their job to track down members of the Belgian resistance, the secret army fighting against the German occupation.

A scene from the invasion of Belgium in May 1940. These refugees are leaving their homes to try and escape the German bombing.

To enforce Nazi rule, the Gestapo and SD interrogators often tortured their prisoners. Torture was allowed under the so-called *Nacht und Nebel* (Night and Fog) order issued by the German leader, Adolf Hitler, in December 1941. This proclaimed that 'enemies of the Reich' could be interrogated by any method and executed without any trial. They were to vanish into the 'night and fog' of the unknown. No information was to be given to their families or relations about their destination or eventual fate.

It took great courage to join or help the resistance. Every day brought the possibility of betrayal by a friend, neighbour or member of your own family. Arrest would result in the interrogation of those closest and

Refugees wander in the streets of Louvain. The effects of the German invasion are shown in the overturned car and the wreckage behind it.

dearest to you. No one was safe. One family directly involved in the resistance was the Daman family, whose home was in the town of Louvain outside Brussels. Jacques Daman was a master shoemaker, his wife Stephanie ran a small grocer's shop from the house where they lived. Two of their four children, their son Francois and daughter Hortense, were members of the resistance.

Francois, who had been a sergeant in the Belgian army, had joined the Belgian Army of Partisans (BAP), which was run by communists. Francois had avoided being sent to Germany as a forced labourer and was now a man on the run. In the summer of 1942 he recruited Hortense, a bright, red-headed young girl of 15, into the BAP. Francois told Hortense that the BAP was not like an ordinary army: *'There aren't any uniforms or camps… but the partisans are well-organized. They have divided everyone into cells, and the idea is that a person in one cell has no connection with a person in another. No one knows what the others have done, or are going to do.'* [2]

Hortense began her life in the resistance as a courier, carrying messages, and then weapons and explosives, to resistance cells. She concealed them under the groceries she delivered in a basket on her bicycle. A courier's life was busy, dangerous and sometimes extremely short. Couriers needed luck as well as courage to survive. Hortense had a steady nerve and an ability to exploit her seeming youthful innocence, which got her out of the tight spots into which her resistance work took her.

Breendonk prison
At the grim fort of Breendonk near Brussels, the Belgian capital, prisoners were held in foul-smelling underground chambers, crammed 60 to a small room, and fed a starvation diet. They worked 12 hours a day at heavy manual labour, guarded by members of the Belgian SS. They could expect no mercy from their fellow countrymen. Victims being interrogated were hung on a pulley block, or tortured with thumbscrews, head vices, electric needles or red-hot iron bars. When they were of no further use to their German captors, they were shot. During the war over 3,500 people died at Breendonk.

German troops outside a Gestapo headquarters. Here prisoners would have been interrogated, possibly using torture.

Hortense ran terrifying risks. In July 1943, she was stopped at a German road block while carrying hand grenades in her basket hidden under a layer of eggs. A German officer bore down on her. Discovery would have meant death. It required all of Hortense's self-control to distract the officer by bribing her way to safety with two of her eggs, which were very scarce items in Belgium in 1943. When Hortense got home, she had to be helped off her bicycle, she was so shocked.

Hortense took part in many other operations. She helped shot-down Allied airmen along the escape lines set up by the resistance. She acted as a look-out when the BAP killed a Belgian who had collaborated with the Nazis (during the war the BAP killed over 1,000 collaborators). Hortense became a hardened professional, highly attuned to the threat of danger. Often she abandoned a meeting or a mission when her instincts told her that something was wrong.

Papers, please: a checkpoint between German-occupied France and the two-fifths of the country which after 1940 was controlled by a puppet French government based in Vichy. Such checkpoints were common throughout Occupied Europe, and it was through one very like this that Hortense Daman smuggled a cargo of hand grenades.

Eventually Hortense's luck ran out. On the night of 14 February 1944 German soldiers and SD men burst into the Damans' home. Hortense became a prisoner of the SS. She was beaten and tortured before being taken to a women's prison not far from her home in Louvain. From there she was regularly taken to the SS interrogation centre, where she suffered more beatings. Shortly after her arrest she was joined in the women's prison by her mother. An Allied air raid on Louvain blasted a gaping hole in the prison wall, giving Hortense a chance to escape. But she feared the revenge the SS might take on her mother and stayed in the prison.

Two days later mother and daughter were separated. Hortense was taken to the main prison in Brussels. On her cell door was a sign that said Condemned to Death. She was still only 17 years old. In solitary confinement she kept in touch with events in the outside world by listening to the messages in Morse code tapped out on the prison's piping system.

At the end of June 1944 Hortense was taken in shackles from the prison and put aboard a train travelling east. The destination was the concentration camp for women at Ravensbruck in Germany. In this hellish place German doctors deliberately injected Hortense with gangrene as part of a terrible medical experiment. She was also subjected to a massive dose of X-rays as part of a sterilization programme. For weeks she lay at death's door in filthy conditions. Somehow she pulled through, saved by her youth and strength of character and the tiny amounts of food her mother – who had also been sent to Ravensbruck – shared with her.

Nearly 90,000 women died at Ravensbruck. Hortense and her mother survived, They lived by their wits amid scenes of terrible suffering and random death. One day Hortense watched as 700 Jewish children from Hungary were gassed to death in a sealed tent.

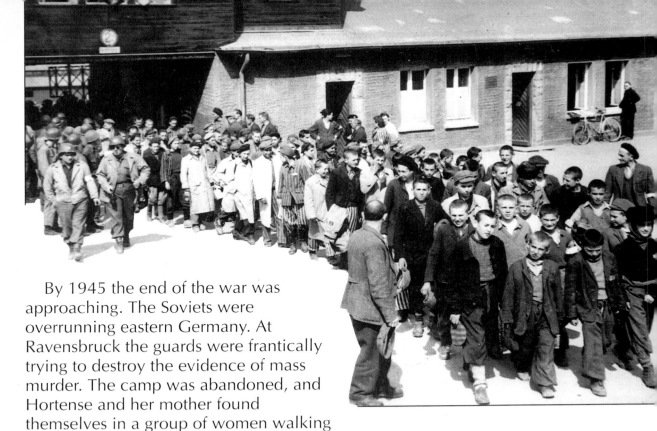

By 1945 the end of the war was approaching. The Soviets were overrunning eastern Germany. At Ravensbruck the guards were frantically trying to destroy the evidence of mass murder. The camp was abandoned, and Hortense and her mother found themselves in a group of women walking westward. They were little more than skeletons. They were rescued by the Swedish Red Cross, and after many adventures reached Denmark.

Hortense and Stephanie were reunited with their family in June 1945, nearly two months after the end of the war in Europe. All had survived. Francois had not been captured by the SS, and at the end of the war he had rescued his father from the concentration camp at Buchenwald near Weimar in Germany.

In February 1946 Hortense married a British serviceman who was stationed in Louvain. Later they settled in England. Her ordeal at Ravensbruck did not prevent Hortense from having children of her own, but it took her many years to fully recover from the experiences she suffered at the hands of the Germans and some of her fellow Belgian citizens. During the war she had progressed from innocent schoolgirl to resistance fighter and concentration camp survivor. She paid a high price for the great courage she had shown.

Some of the young survivors of the Buchenwald concentration camp begin their journey to freedom in May 1945. Francois Daman rescued his father from the camp when it was liberated on 13 April 1945.

Under fire

At the beginning of May 1941 the German bombing campaign against Britain's cities, known as the Blitz, was coming to an end. But before turning his air force against the Soviet Union, Adolf Hitler made one last effort to bomb Britain off the map.

On the night of 7 May one of the German targets was Bootle, an industrial town in Lancashire in north-west England. The attack on Bootle was so heavy and destructive that the telephone links between the town's Fire Service headquarters and its outlying depots were cut. Signals had to be carried to and fro by bicycle messengers.

A rescue squad and civilian helpers fight to free people trapped under the rubble of a bombed building after a German air raid. Bombing of cities meant that the Second World War was the first in which large numbers of civilians were threatened by death.

One of the messengers was 16-year-old Ronald Heys. The bombs were still falling as Ronald set off to deliver his first message. He pedalled through blazing streets strewn with rubble. The road ahead was carpeted with shards of glass from shop windows broken by explosions. The tyres of his bike were punctured and Ronald was thrown off. Undaunted, Ronald delivered the message on foot with his bike slung around his shoulders, then turned and headed for home still carrying it.

Once the message had been safely delivered and Ronald had returned to the Fire Service headquarters, he was immediately sent out again. Taking a second bike, Ronald set off into the inferno. He had not gone far when he rode straight into a wrecked vehicle. His bike was destroyed by the collision, so for a second time that evening Ronald delivered his message on foot, running all the way.

No sooner had he arrived back at headquarters than Ronald was given a third message and a third bike. As he hurried on his way a bomb exploded dead ahead of him: Ronald catapulted into the crater the bomb had made in the road. Ronald clambered out of the smouldering hole and, leaving behind a smashed bike for a third time in the same evening, ran on to deliver his message.

Ronald's night was not yet over. On his return to headquarters, bruised, battered and exhausted, Ronald was handed another message and another bike. Off he went, but this time his luck ran out. A bomb exploded close by, knocking him unconscious. When Ronald came to, his only thought was to deliver his message. This time his bike had survived the blast, but Ronald had an ugly wound in his leg. Nevertheless, Ronald pushed the bike all the way to deliver his message and then returned to base. When he limped into the Fire Service headquarters, his first words were, 'Any more messages, sir?' For his bravery that night Ronald was awarded the British Empire Medal.

'Beat Firebomb Fritz: Britain shall not burn': a confident prediction, but German firebombs still caused widespread damage in many of Britain's cities. Enemy bombing raids also destroyed large areas of other cities all round the world.

24

A Hitler Youth unit on parade in 1934. By 1939 virtually every young German male between the ages of ten and eighteen was a member of the Hitler Youth. It gave boys military training and used camps and rallies to ensure they held Nazi beliefs. The female equivalent was the League of German Girls, which stressed the importance of traditional female roles – home-making and child-rearing.

By 1943 Germany's cities were under heavy attack from RAF Bomber Command. On the night of 24 July the city of Hamburg was attacked by nearly 800 British bombers. The city's civil defence system was overwhelmed, its communications wrecked and the streets blocked. A huge firestorm, ten kilometres square, engulfed the centre of the city.

Fifteen-year-old Herbert Brecht was a member of one of the fire service's *Schellkommandos*, small squads whose task it was to rush to the scene of a fire. There was little that Herbert's squad could do in the furnace of the firestorm. Later Herbert recalled: *'I was in the wooden trailer with two other lads. The heat from the surrounding houses which were on fire was unbearable. We whimpered and cried from the pain of it… Burning people ran and staggered after us. Others were lying on the road, dead or unconscious. At the junction of Suderstrasse and Louisenweg, our trailer got stuck in a bomb crater. We unhitched it and jumped into the car, which was still running; there were six of us crammed inside. After another 200 metres we were forced to a halt… Our car caught fire immediately. We all managed to get out and we stood there in those fires of hell.'* [3]

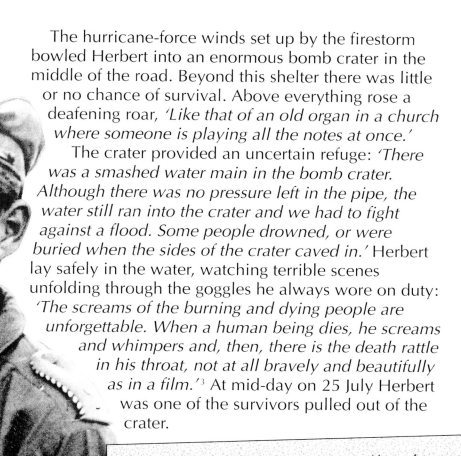

The hurricane-force winds set up by the firestorm bowled Herbert into an enormous bomb crater in the middle of the road. Beyond this shelter there was little or no chance of survival. Above everything rose a deafening roar, *'Like that of an old organ in a church where someone is playing all the notes at once.'*

The crater provided an uncertain refuge: *'There was a smashed water main in the bomb crater. Although there was no pressure left in the pipe, the water still ran into the crater and we had to fight against a flood. Some people drowned, or were buried when the sides of the crater caved in.'* Herbert lay safely in the water, watching terrible scenes unfolding through the goggles he always wore on duty: *'The screams of the burning and dying people are unforgettable. When a human being dies, he screams and whimpers and, then, there is the death rattle in his throat, not at all bravely and beautifully as in a film.'*[3] At mid-day on 25 July Herbert was one of the survivors pulled out of the crater.

Herbert's rescuer was an elderly man whose face was badly burned. **'When he pulled me out by the hands, my skin stuck to him in shreds. He looked at me – I cannot describe his look – and he could only say, "Junge, Junge" (Young, Young). I cannot say how many survived in that crater. I had been given a new, brown uniform only three weeks earlier and been told that it was flame-resistant. I feel that this saved my life. My old uniform had been a captured French soldier's uniform with some old First World War boots.'**[3]

A member of the Hitler Youth. During the war its members played an increasingly important part on the German home front, replacing the young men who had been called up by the armed forces. By the end of the war many boys of the Hitler Youth were also pressed into the front line as last-ditch defenders of Germany.

Young boy-soldiers dressed in uniforms made for men: these boys survived the fighting and were captured in Nuremberg at the end of the war.

The Volkssturm

In April 1945 one veteran German soldier watched a *Volkssturm* detachment spilling out of a factory yard in East Prussia. 'Some of these soldiers with Mausers (rifles) on their shoulders must have been at least 60 or 65... But the young boys were even more astonishing... They had been hastily dressed in worn uniforms cut for men, and were carrying guns which were often as big as they were... We noticed some heart-wringing details about these children, who were beginning the first day of their tragedy. Several of them were carrying school satchels their mothers had packed with extra food and clothes instead of schoolbooks. A few of the boys were trading the sweets which the rations allowed the children under 13.' From *Forgotten Soldier* by Guy Fager.

By 1943 Germany's shrinking reserves of manpower meant that teenage boys and girls played an increasingly important part in the defence of its cities against Allied bombers. To replace the able-bodied men fighting in Russia, 700,000 teenagers of the *Hitlerjugend* (Hitler Youth, the Nazi youth organization) were drafted into civil defence. They served as messengers, telephone operators, hospital orderlies, rescue diggers and, like Herbert Brecht, firefighters. When the time came for 16-year-old anti-aircraft gunners to go into the Army, their place was taken by even younger boys, and teenage girls recruited from the League of German Girls. Searchlights were sometimes operated by 12-year-old boys.

Teenage soldiers formed the core of the 12th SS Panzer Division, drawn from the ranks of the *Hitlerjugend*. In some of the division's battalions over 60 per cent of the soldiers were under 18 years of age. They made up for their youth with fanatical courage. Their baptism of fire came in Normandy in June 1944. A tank commander who fought them recalled that the *Hitlerjugend* sprang at Allied tanks *'like young wolves, until we were forced to kill them against our will.'*

By the end of the war the remnants of Hitler's Third Reich was in large part defended by the old men and young boys of the *Volkssturm*. Formed in the autumn of 1944, the *Volkssturm* supposedly contained all males between the ages of 16 and 60 who were not in the armed forces but were capable of bearing arms. In fact, many of its members were under 16.

Riding bicycles and armed with hand-held *Panzerfaust* anti-tank guns, these boys were sent into the last-ditch battle to save the Reich. Many were determined to fight, even though there was nothing left to defend. A US tank commander recalled an incident in Austria in the closing days of the war: *'The world of these children of the Hitler Youth was coming to an end. Soon there would be nothing left. No parades, no songs, no swastikas, no marching and no fighting for their Faith – for the belief in Hitler… There was one boy we took prisoner. His rocket had hit my tank but had not exploded. I was livid that this snotty brat should endanger my life and I was out of that tank very quickly, cuffing him about the head and shouting. When I let go of him he fell to the grass crying and saying something. I do not speak German but my sergeant did. What the child was saying was that he should have died for the Führer… he was sorry that he had not been killed knocking out my tank.'* (From *Last Days of the Reich* by James Lucas.)

As the war in Europe draws to a close a young German boy is taught to use a Panzerfaust *(Tankfist) anti-tank gun. It was tucked under the arm and aimed, then fired at a tank. Later models had a range of about 150 metres.*

Children of the Holocaust

Julius Streicher, who was one of Hitler's earliest supporters. Even by the standards of the Nazis he was a violent, evil man, and by 1940 he had been stripped of his official jobs. After the war Streicher was convicted of crimes against humanity and hanged. To the very end he gloried in his self-conferred nickname of Jew-Baiter.

In the 1930s the Nazis had excluded the Jews in Germany from society. By the autumn of 1942 Adolf Hitler, the German leader, controlled an empire that stretched from the shores of the Atlantic to the Caucasus Mountains in the USSR. These conquered territories contained large Jewish populations. In January 1942 the Nazis had decided to exterminate them systematically. They called this decision the 'Final Solution to the Jewish Problem'. It is now often called the Holocaust. During the Second World War they killed at least six million Jews, of whom as many as 1.5 million were children.

The fate of the Jewish children was sealed from the start. The Nazis were not content with killing their parents. All the Jews had to be killed. Only then could Europe be 'Jew-free'.

The killing began before January 1942. When the Germans invaded the USSR in June 1941, the Army was followed by SS *Einsatzgruppen* (Operation Groups). These were mobile murder squads whose orders were to kill all the Jews they could find. Thousands of Jewish children died alongside their parents, rounded up and then machine-gunned on the edge of ditches or freshly dug trenches.

A 1942 photograph of a group of Yugoslavians on their way to an unknown fate at the hands of the Germans. Yugoslavia was invaded by Germany in the spring of 1941. Later the Germans kidnapped many Yugoslavian children for the Lebensborn *programme.*

Other methods of mass destruction were employed. In the towns and cities of Eastern Europe the Jews were herded into ghettos, areas that were walled off from the rest of the population. Inside the ghettos thousands died from disease and hunger. Josef Goebbels, the Nazi propaganda minister, called them 'death boxes'. The largest ghetto was in Warsaw, in Poland. Inside its walls were packed nearly half a million Jews, of whom 150,000 were children under the age of 15.

Inside the ghettos, the Jewish authorities struggled to provide something like a normal life for the children. But there were no schools, and no parks or playgrounds. There were no trees to climb and not a patch of grass to play on. On every street corner were huddled groups of small children in rags, swollen from hunger and ravaged by disease.

The Lebensborn

The Lebensborn (Spring of Life) programme was conceived by the chief of the SS, Heinrich Himmler. Its aim was to transform the German nation into a super-race by selective breeding. The Nazis believed that it was important for women to bear as many sound children as possible. The Nazis did not mind if children were born to unmarried mothers. These received good treatment before and after the birth in special Lebensborn clinics.

During the war the Lebensborn programme was extended to embrace the kidnapping of children in occupied Europe to add to the breeding stock of the Third Reich. 'Racially acceptable' children were taken from Poland, France, Norway and Czechoslovakia and 'Germanized' in children's homes or with German families. On Himmler's orders children were selected in mass examinations and then torn from their families. Several thousand children were caught up in this programme, many of them from Poland.

Children in the Warsaw Ghetto in 1941. Thousands had to fend for themselves on the streets after their parents had died or been sent to concentration camps.

In the summer of 1940 Mary Berg, a 16-year-old girl who lived in the ghetto, wrote in her diary: *'There are a great number of almost naked children whose parents have died, and who sit in rags in the streets. Their bodies are horribly emaciated; one can see the bones through the parchment-yellow skin. This is the first sign of scurvy; in the last stages of this terrible disease the same little bodies are blown up and covered with festering wounds. Some of the children have lost their toes. They toss around and groan. They no longer have a human appearance and are more like monkeys than children. They no longer beg for bread but for death.'*

The soup kitchens and dusty little playgrounds set up in the ghettos by the Jewish authorities could not end the suffering, but only prolong it. The small children of the ghetto grew up with the sight and smell of death all around them. People collapsed and died in the streets and were left where they fell. In one courtyard in the Lodz ghetto, in Poland, the small children played a game called 'tickling the corpse'.

In regular raids called *Kinderaktionen* (Child Actions), German troops would enter the ghettos to round up pregnant women and children. They were then transported to death camps set up by the Germans in eastern Europe for the mass extermination of the Jews. Sometimes the children of the ghetto would play their own version of the *Kinderaktionen*, with the older, stronger ones taking the part of the Germans and the younger ones attempting to hide from them as the Jews.

The *Kinderaktionen* were carried out across Europe, from the Ukraine to France. No one was safe. In the small French town of Isieux 44 children from a children's home were tossed into trucks 'like packages' by men of the Gestapo (German secret police). One was set free because he was not Jewish. The rest were sent to the death camp at Auschwitz in southern Poland.

On their eastward journey many of the Jewish mothers and children of western Europe passed through the transit camp at Theresienstadt (now called Terezin) in Czechoslovakia. Here the camp commandant provided a basic system of child care. Thousands of drawings made by children at Theresienstadt survived the war. They provide a reminder of the young lives the Nazis destroyed.

Child Smugglers of the Ghetto

Small Jewish children risked their lives smuggling desperately needed food into the Warsaw ghetto: 'Once again we can observe the scores of Jewish children from the age of 10 to 12 or 13 stealing over to the Aryan side to buy a few potatoes there. These they hide in their little coats, with hems swollen so that the children look like balloons. Whole hosts of them can be seen climbing over the (ghetto) walls... There are some Germans who show a little mercy for these unfortunate children and pretend not to see... There are also vicious guards who hit the children with murderous blows, take away their potatoes and often even use their weapons. More than one child has fallen victim to their bloodlust. These poor unfortunate Jewish children! What wonderful human potential is being lost to us.' From the diary of Abraham Lewin, 22 May 1942.

Starving within sight of food, two children in the Warsaw Ghetto sit outside a shop.

One by one the ghettos were cleared and the Jews sent to the death camps. Crammed into cattle trucks, many children died on the journey. On arrival at Auschwitz the smaller children and their mothers were immediately murdered in the camp's gas chambers. The camp's commandant Rudolf Hoess later explained the reason: *'Children of tender years were invariably exterminated since by reason of their youth they were unable to work.'* Only those who were tall enough to pass as adults were spared for any length of time.

Unaware of their fate, the little ones often played games at the very doors of the gas chambers. Even Hoess was affected by such scenes. Tried after the war for crimes against humanity, he testified: *'Once two little children were so engrossed in their play that they did not want to be torn away from it by their mother… I will never forget the pleading look of the mother, begging for mercy though she certainly knew what was going to happen.'*

Sometimes people were not killed in the systematic way they were at Auschwitz. Instead they were starved and worked to death. In 1944 at Ravensbruck, the camp for women where Hortense Daman was imprisoned, there were about 500 children. One inmate left a vivid description of the older ones: *'They looked like skeletons wearing rags. Some had no hair on their heads. Nevertheless they behaved like children, running around and begging things from their elders. They even played games. A popular one was Appel, modelled on the camp's daily roll calls.'*[4]

Diary of a Young Girl

During the war some Jewish children lived in hiding. In 1933 the Frank family fled from Germany when the Nazis came to power. They settled in Holland, but after Germany occupied Holland in 1940 they lived in constant danger of being sent to the concentration camps. The family went into hiding in the backroom office of a warehouse in July 1942. Neighbours fed and protected them until they were betrayed by an informer in August 1944. The Franks were sent to the concentration camp at Belsen in Germany. Only the father survived. After the war he discovered the diary that had been kept by his teenage daughter Anne during their period of hiding. She had died of typhus at Belsen in March 1945. The diary is moving proof of Anne's optimism and love of life in even the most difficult circumstances. In her diary she wrote, *'In spite of everything I still believe that people are really good at heart.'*

The daily roll call sometimes lasted for hours. Even the dead had to be brought out for it. The children stood through it alongside the adults. On one occasion a woman gave birth in the middle of *Appel* without anyone being allowed to offer her the slightest help.

Until 1944 children born in Ravensbruck were drowned in a bucket of water or destroyed in the camp's gas chambers, a process which could take up to 30 minutes as the young were more resistant to the gas. Genevieve de Gaulle, a prisoner at Ravensbruck, wrote: *'For most of the time the small children of Ravensbruck were lying completely exhausted on their miserable camp mattresses, they were breathing in the foul air of the barracks, awaiting far too quietly the return of their mothers if they were privileged not to be separated from them. It was a dangerous thing to linger about on the camp roadways. In the same way as the parents, they were just as likely to be beaten.'*[4]

Young boys who had been prisoners at the Dachau concentration camp cheer the US troops who liberated them.

At some of the camps terrible medical experiments were carried out on small children. At Auschwitz the camp doctor, Josef Mengele, conducted horrifying experiments on twins. It is estimated that about two million people died at Auschwitz before it was closed in 1944. The horrors at Ravensbruck continued until the last weeks of the war in Europe. Not all of those responsible for these crimes were brought to justice after the war. Mengele escaped to South America. He managed to stay one step ahead of his pursuers until he died in 1984.

Children of Hiroshima

By the spring of 1945 it was clear that Japan had lost the war. US submarines had sunk the merchant ships which carried the food and fuel it needed to continue the fight. Its navy had been destroyed by the US carrier fleet. Japan's large cities had been devastated by B-29 Superfortress heavy bombers, and its people were on the verge of starvation.

The bombing had come to Japan late in the war. The US advance across the Pacific did not bring their land-based bombers within range of the Japanese home islands until the end of 1944. But the Japanese knew what Allied bombers had done to the cities of Germany and had prepared for the onslaught. One of the measures they took was to evacuate 450,000 children from their major cities.

One of the children evacuated into the Japanese countryside was 11-year-old Sato Hideo. During the closing months of the war there was little time for school-work as Japan prepared for an invasion by the Allies: *'The main thing we did was to dig an anti-tank ditch in the corner of the schoolyard. "Dig a hole", they told us. The older children were no longer around. From April 1945 on everyone above us was mobilized daily for work in war plants, while we spent days in "octopus" holes. That was terrible work for an elementary schoolkid. It took three days just to hollow out a single foxhole deep enough so that when the teacher jumped in it would be over his head.'*[5]

Above: A street in Hiroshima before the war. Below: The same street after the dropping of an atomic bomb on the city in August 1945.

There was to be no invasion. The US President, Harry S Truman, had been told by his military chiefs that an invasion of Japan would cost the Allies up to a million casualties. He decided to use a new weapon to bring an end to the war – the atomic bomb, which had been successfully tested in the New Mexico desert on 16 July 1945. The target selected by the USA for the first atomic bomb attack was Hiroshima, a medium-sized city on the edge of Japan's Inland Sea, which had large military and supply depots, shipyards and industrial plants. Its population of about 380,000 had been reduced to less than 300,000 by evacuation and the demolition of some 70,000 houses. These had been knocked down to create firebreaks designed to stop fires spreading rapidly through the city. However, the centre of Hiroshima was still densely populated.

By the last year of the war, Allied fighter-bombers were ranging over the Japanese countryside at will, shooting at everything that moved. For Sato Hideo and his friends these deadly missions became part of an extraordinary game with death. Sometimes they were sent into the fields to cut grass to feed military horses: 'We'd scatter in all directions at the shout "They're coming", trying to get into the woods. If you were too far from the trees, first you'd run with your back to the plane. Then you'd turn to face it. Bullets stretched out towards you in a line. You'd try to get your body between these streams of bullets. You'd just throw yourself flat, and raise your head and watch the plane... The instant you knew they'd missed you'd stand up and start running... They were so slow that the pilot opened his cockpit window and leaned out – American pilots looking at us wearing airplane goggles. I even waved at them.'[5]

The USA's first blow from the sky against Japan. On 18 April 1942, 16 US bombers took off from the aircraft carrier Hornet to attack targets 1,300 kilometres away in Tokyo, Kobe, Yokohama and Nagoya. Later in the war US aircraft constantly flew over Japan.

At 7.09 on the sunny Monday morning of 6 August 1945 the air raid siren sounded over Hiroshima. But the people already at work or those hurrying to work took little notice. All seemed well when about half an hour later the all-clear sounded. But disaster on an unimaginable scale was only minutes away. At around 8.15 a single B-29 Superfortress dropped an atomic bomb on Hiroshima from a height of 9,500 metres above the city. Forty-three seconds later the bomb exploded 600 metres above the ground near a bridge over the Ota river.

Immediately underneath the explosion the ground temperature was at least 5,000 °C. Thousands of people were instantly vapourized. Farther away from the centre of the blast buildings were flattened by the shock, burying thousands more under the wreckage. Tramcars and trains were tossed through the air like toys. Trees and grass caught fire.

Little girls at a Japanese school are trained in the martial arts.

Children of Japan
From the 1930s Japanese schoolchildren had been educated in a military atmosphere, but now there was an extra edge to the daily routine. The evacuated children rose at 6am, assembled in squads in front of their sleeping quarters and bowed in the direction of the Japanese emperor's palace. They then chanted, 'We are the children of the divine country Japan. We are the children of fighting Japan which is building Greater East Asia.'

High school boy Iwao Nakamura saw terrible things on the day the atomic bomb exploded in Hiroshima. He remembered that after the bomb exploded *'it became as dark as night... flames shooting up from* wrecked houses as if to illuminate the darkness. Amidst this were children aimlessly wandering about, groaning with pain, their burned faces twitching and bloated like balloons.'[6]

Six-year-old Shigeko Hirata saw *'many people running from the centre of the city. They all looked the same. Their skin was burned off and was dangling from their hands and chins. Their faces were red and so swollen that they didn't seem to have any eyes or mouths. In the direction of the city we could see a large column of black smoke climbing into the sky. It was a horrible sight. I was scared and shook as I hung on to Mother. Then Daddy came running up to us with a horrible look on his face. He had a cut on his hip. The colour was terrible, something between yellow and black. His hair was full of ashes. As we ran for safety we saw people become too tired to walk another step and fall by the roadside.'[6]*

Two days after the destruction of Hiroshima, Japanese Navy doctors give first aid to survivors at one of the few large buildings left standing in the city.

Along with his family, Shigeko joined the thousands of dazed survivors streaming out of Hiroshima. They passed by a primary school: *'I saw a damaged water tank in which a number of people had their heads down drinking. I was so thirsty… that I left my parents' side without thinking and approached the tank. But when I got near and was able to see into the tank I gave an involuntary cry and backed away. What I saw reflected in the blood-stained water was the faces of monsters. They had leaned over the side of the tank and died in that position. From the burned shreds of their sailor uniforms I knew they were schoolgirls.'*[6]

Hiroshima from a distance
Many of Tokyo's students and older children were working in war factories on the outskirts of Hiroshima and escaped the full effect of the blast. Kazuko Komae, a middle-school pupil who had been evacuated to a village 21 kilometres outside Tokyo, saw the tragedy unfold from a distance: *'A bluish-white flare many times as bright as the sun and then a deafening explosion. In an instant the sky was overcast with black smoke. I took shelter behind the hill at the back of the temple which served as a school building. There I found many people, their pale faces together whispering, "Hiroshima has been destroyed."'*[6]

A shack amid the devastation of postwar Japan. By the end of the war one in four Japanese people did not have adequate housing.

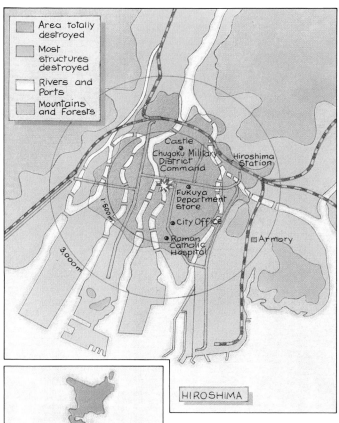

Castle
Chugoku Military
District
Command
Hiroshima
Station
Fukuya
Department
store
City Office
Roman
Catholic
Hospital
Armory
1,500m
3,000m
HIROSHIMA

These maps show the areas affected by the 1945 atomic explosions in Hiroshima and Nagasaki.

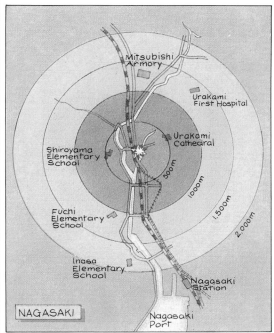

Mitsubishi
Armory
Urakami
First Hospital
Shiroyama
Elementary
School
Urakami
Cathedral
Fuchi
Elementary
School
500m
1,000m
1,500m
2,000m
Inasa
Elementary
School
Nagasaki
Station
Nagasaki
Port
NAGASAKI

TOKYO
HIROSHIMA
NAGASAKI
JAPAN

In Hiroshima black raindrops the size of marbles were beginning to fall. This was the vapourized moisture from the fireball of the explosion as it condensed into a vast mushroom cloud which rose above the city and then cooled. The raindrops contained radiation which penetrated deep into the marrow of human bones. Many people who survived the atomic explosion apparently physically unharmed would later die of radiation sickness. Among them was Shigeko Hirata's father. Shigeko recalled that *'the cuts on my feet were slow to heal... and took a whole year to get better.'* About a month after the attack five-year-old Yukiharu Suzuki got *'sores all over me and all my hair fell out. No one thought I was going to live but they all took good care of me and I gradually got better... We all went to see our house, but there was nothing left but burned ground.'* [6]

41

Some children were not so lucky. For many of the full effects of the radiation sickness did not appear until years later. In January 1951 11-year-old Ikuko Wakasa wrote: *'Only six months ago, a ten-year-old girl lost all her hair from radiation sickness. The Red Cross hospital doctors did their best to help her but she vomited blood and died in 20 days.'*[6]

It has been estimated that up to 270,000 citizens of Hiroshima were either killed outright by the atomic bomb or died within five years of radiation sickness. Up to 87,000 people died as the result of a second atomic bomb attack on the city of Nagasaki on 9 August. Japan formally surrendered to the Allies on 2 September 1945.

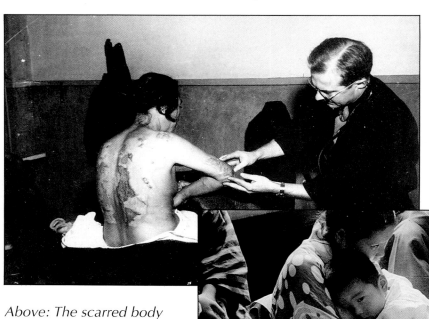

Below: Women and children queue for medical treatment in Hiroshima in 1946.

Above: The scarred body of Tama Umada in October 1946. Tama suffered severe burns when standing about one and a half kilometres from the centre of the atomic blast at Nagasaki.

Teenagers in America

Unlike children and adolescents in Europe and the Far East, the young of the United States were not caught up in Total War. They did not experience the mixture of fear and excitement which young Londoners felt in an air raid. Nor did they see the terrible results of bombing. They did not endure semi-starvation, as millions of children did. Nor were they forced into battle like the boy soldiers of Germany.

In Europe and Asia the war brought devastation and suffering on a colossal scale. In the United States the war brought a new prosperity to Americans emerging from the economic slump of the 1930s. Agriculture and industry boomed as the United States supplied its allies with huge quantities of weapons and food, and also mobilized its own forces for the war in the Pacific and Europe. The new prosperity produced a new kind of adolescent in America - the teenager.

A young zoot suiter shows off his strange clothing in 1939.

Because their parents were better off and many of them had part-time jobs, teenagers had money to spend. For the first time they wielded economic power, and magazines like *Seventeen* catered for their interest in clothes, movies and music.

The 'jive talk' they used amongst themselves, much influenced by pop singers like the young Frank Sinatra, baffled adults, as it was meant to do. Magazines like Life devoted lengthy articles to teenage fashions.

The word teenager first came into general use in the USA during the Second World War. Most young people between the ages of 14 and 18 were at high school. They were not directly involved in war work, and would not be called up to serve in the armed forces or war factories until they were 18. In between childhood and adulthood they created their own identity.

With so many over-18s away on war service, teenagers became a more noticeable group. Not all the attention they attracted was welcome. Throughout the war there was much public alarm about the growth of a new social problem - juvenile delinquency. During the last nine months of the war in Indianapolis juveniles accounted for 65 per cent of all arrests by the police. Much of this was blamed on wartime upheavals. With fathers away in the forces and mothers doing full-time war work, people were afraid that teenagers were running wild. In Los Angeles in June 1943 there were riots following clashes between servicemen and the flamboyantly dressed members of teenage Mexican-American gangs. The teenagers were wearing zoot suits, which were also popular with many young blacks and poor urban whites. The zoot suit consisted of a pancake hat, long drape jacket heavily padded at the shoulders, narrow-cuffed trousers and thick-soled shoes. The zoot suiter completed the effect with hair slicked back into a ducktail at the back. The Los Angeles city authorities were so alarmed by the zoot suit phenomenon that they attempted to ban the wearing of them inside the city limits.

Jitterbug dancers in New York in 1941, when the dance was all the rage in America.

Timeline

1929   October 29th Wall Street Crash, triggers Great Depression.
1931   April 14th Spain becomes a republic.
1933   January 30th Hitler appointed Chancellor of Germany. August 2nd Hitler becomes Führer (German dictator).
1935   October 2nd Italian troops invade Ethiopia.
1936   February Popular Front wins elections in Spain.
March 8th German troops enter Rhineland.
July 18th Rebellion by army officers begins Spanish Civil War.
November 1st Italy and Germany sign Rome-Berlin Axis.
1937   July 7th Japan attacks China. November 6th Italy, Germany and Japan sign the Anti-Comintern Pact.
1938   March 12th Anschluss (union of Germany and Austria) declared: German troops occupy Austria.
August-September International confrontation over Hitler's demands for part of Czechoslovakia (the Sudetenland).
September 30th Munich Conference resolves Czech crisis.
October 12th German troops occupy Sudetenland.

1939
March 12th German forces occupy Czechoslovakia. 28th Franco's forces capture Madrid: Spanish Civil War ends. 31st France and Britain guarantee Polish independence.
May 2nd Germany and Italy agree Pact of Steel alliance. August 23rd USSR-German non-aggression pact agreed. September 1st Germany invades western Poland. 3rd France and Britain declare war on Germany. 17th Soviet troops invade eastern Poland.

1940
April 7th Norway and Denmark attacked by Germany. May 10th German troops begin invasion of Netherlands, Belgium and Luxembourg. Churchill becomes British prime minister. 12th Germany begins invasion of France.
June 10th Italy declares war on Britain and France.
14th German forces capture Paris. 22nd French sign armistice at Compiégne. Battle of Britain begins.
September 27th Germany, Italy and Japan sign the Tripartite Pact. November 5th Roosevelt re-elected US president. 14th Coventry, England, levelled by German bombers.

1941
March 11th Lend-Lease Act signed. April 17th Germany starts invasion of Balkans and Greece. June 22nd Invasion of USSR by Germany (Operation Barbarossa) begins.
July US embargoes on oil and steel exports to Japan.
August 14th Roosevelt and Churchill sign Atlantic Charter, agreeing war aims.
November German forces halted outside Moscow.

December 7th Japan bombs US naval base at Pearl Harbor, Hawaii. Japan declares war on USA.
8th USA and Britain declare war on Japan.
11th Germany and Italy declare war on USA: USA declares war on them.

1942
February 15th Singapore captured by Japanese. April 9th US forces on Bataan Peninsula surrender. May 6th US forces on Corregidor surrender. July Battle of Stalingrad begins.
November 8th US and British troops land in North Africa. 11th German forces enter Vichy France.

1943
January 14-24th Casablanca Conference agrees Allied war aim of unconditional enemy surrender. February 2nd German army at Stalingrad surrenders. May 12th War ends in North Africa. July 10th Allied forces land in Sicily.
26th Mussolini resigns. September 3rd Allies land in Italy. 8th Italy surrenders. 10th Nazi forces occupy Rome. November 22-25th Cairo Conference.
28th Tehran Conference opens.

1944
March Soviet troops re-enter Poland.
June 4th Allied troops enter Rome.
6th D-day: Allied invasion of France begins. July 20th Hitler wounded in assassination attempt by German officers. 21st Dumbarton Oaks Conference lays down basis for United Nations. August Warsaw Uprising starts. 25th Paris liberated. October Warsaw Uprising crushed. 6th Soviet forces enter Hungary and Czechoslovakia. 20th US forces enter Philippines.
November All-out US bombing of Japan begins.
December 16th German troops attack through Ardennes.

1945
February 4th Yalta conference.
April 1st US forces occupy Okinawa.
12th Roosevelt dies: Truman US president. 20th Soviet forces enter Berlin. 28th Mussolini executed. May 1st Hitler's suicide announced in Berlin. 2nd Berlin captured. 7th Germany signs unconditional surrender.
June 26th UN formed. July 17th Potsdam conference opens. August 6th Atomic bomb dropped on Hiroshima. 8th Atomic bomb dropped on Nagasaki.
September 2nd Japan signs surrender.

1946   March 5th Churchill's 'Iron Curtain' speech.
1947   March 12th Truman Doctrine outlined.
June 5th Marshall Plan put forward.
1948   June 24th USSR begins blockade of West Berlin (ends May12th 1949).

Glossary

All-clear   A siren that was sounded during the war to let people know that the danger of an air raid was past.

Anti-semitism   A general and illogical dislike of someone who is Jewish.

British Dominions   Countries that were once colonies of Britain but are now independent.

Cells   Small, self-contained units. In the resistance, cells were small groups of a few people who worked together.

Civil Defence   A civilian organization for dealing with disasters, especially air raids.

Class   A way of distinguishing one section of society from another. It recognizes working class, middle class and upper class: generally, working class people are poorer and upper class people are wealthier. Wealth is not the only measure of class: it includes the way people speak, where they went to school, what their parents do for a living and where they were born.

Coalition government   A government made up of people from more than one political party.

Concentration camp   A place in which political prisoners and outlaws are kept. In Nazi Germany the camps were filled with Jews, homosexuals, gypsys and other groups the Nazis hated.

Exodus   A movement of a huge number of people from one place to another. One famous exodus is recorded in the Christian Bible, in which Moses led the whole people of Israel out of Egypt in their search for the Promised Land.

Gangrene   The death and decomposition of a part of the body, usually caused by the flow of blood being obstructed.

Ghetto   Originally the word just meant the Jewish part of a city. During the Second World War the Nazis sealed the ghettos in many European cities and let the people inside starve to death, and ghetto became an unpleasant word. Now it is used to describe any area in which a group of people live in very poor conditions.

Haversack   A kind of strong bag for carrying supplies in.

Inferno   A scene of horror and suffering, especially with fire and dreadful heat. The word is a reference to a book by an Italian writer named Dante, whose book *The Inferno* described what Hell was like.

Labour camp   A prison camp in which criminals and prisoners of war are kept and made to work for their captors.

Morals

Morse code   A system of communication in which dots and dashes stand for letters of the alphabet.

NKVD The USSR's secret police.
Partisan See **Resistance**.
Propaganda Information released by an organization for political purposes.
Resistance The name given to the groups that fought against German, Italian or Japanese invasions of their countries. Resistance fighters were also sometimes called partisans, especially in Eastern Europe.
Roll call A register – often taken at the start of the day – of who is present and who is absent.
Sterilization Making someone incapable of having children.
V-weapons A group name for weapons developed in Germany and called *Vergeltungswaffen* (revenge weapons) by Hitler. The V-1 was a flying bomb and the V-2 a guided rocket. Both were fired at Britain from launching sites in Europe.

Films

Several recent films have dealt with the war from a child's point of view. Two of the best are *Empire of the Sun*, an American film which tells of a young European boy's experiences as a prisoner of the Japanese, and *Hope And Glory*, an English film about life for a boy in England during the war. *Schindler's List* is about a man who saved Jewish people from the concentration camps by sheltering them in his factory.

Books to read

My Childhood in Nazi Germany Elspeth Emmerich (Wayland 1991) A personal account of the war by a young girl in Germany in the 1930s and 1940s.
The Second World War Charles Messenger (Franklin Watts 1986) A good general account of the war.
The Second World War edited by Stewart Ross (Wayland 1989). Another good general account of the war, which uses pictures from unusual sources.
Victims of War (Wayland 1993) and *Cities at War* (Wayland 1994), both by Robin Cross, contain more information on the Warsaw Ghetto, how the war affected the USA and the effect of air raids.

Text acknowledgements
You can find out more about some of the personal stories in this book from the following:
1. *A Boy in the Gulag* Jerzy Kmiecik (Quartet, 1983); **2.** *Hortense Daman - Child at War* Mark Bles (Hodder and Stoughton, 1989); Herbert Brecht in **3.** *Under Fire - The Battle of Hamburg* Martin Middlebrook (Penguin 1984); children of the Holocaust in **4.** *Children at Play in the Holocaust* George Eisen (University of Massachusetts Press, 1988); Sato Hideo in **5.** *Japan at War - an Oral History* Haruko and Theodore Cook (New Press, 1992); other Japanese children in **6.** *Children of Hiroshima* (distributed by Taylor and Francis, 4 John Street London WC2 2ET).

Permission to use quotations from the above works has been sought where appropriate, and is gratefully acknowledged.

Index

*Numbers in **bold** refer to text that is accompanied by pictures.*